Mother-Son
Book Club Guide

Building Connection & Community

Meghan Voss

Stefanie Hohl

Playful Learning Press

Mother-Son Book Club Guide
Copyright © 2025 by Meghan Voss and Stefanie Hohl

All rights reserved. Printed in the United States of America.

No part of this book may be used or reproduced in any manner without written permission.

For information regarding permission, go to www.stefaniehohl.com.

Summary: A guide for planning Mother-Son Book Club events including book summaries, discussion questions, snacks, and ideas for activities.

ISBN: 978-1-63824-057-0

Dedication

MV: To my book-loving sons—stay curious!

SH: To my boys and all our Mother-Son Book Club friends

Table of Contents

PART 1: Helpful Information
- Building Connection & Community
- Who Can Use This Book
- What's Included
- Tips for Launching YOUR Book Club
- Tips for Hosts
- Activity Ideas for Any Book
- A Note from the Authors

PART 2: The Guide
- *Ground Zero* by Alan Gratz 13
- *Nathan Hale's Hazardous Tales: One Dead Spy* by Nathan Hale 19
- *Ghost* by Jason Reynolds 25
- *Wonder* by R. J. Palacio 31
- *Fablehaven* by Brandon Mull 37
- *Sal and Gabi Break the Universe* by Carlos Hernandez 43
- *Hatchet* by Gary Paulsen 49
- *New Kid* by Jerry Craft 55
- *Holes* by Louis Sachar 61
- *The Crossover* by Kwame Alexander 67
- *The Boy Who Harnessed the Wind, Young Readers Edition* by William Kamkwamba 73
- *All Thirteen: The Incredible Cave Rescue of the Thai Boys' Soccer Team* by Christina Soontornvat 79

APPENDIX
- Index
- About the Authors

PART I
Helpful Information

Part 1: Helpful Information

Book Clubs:
Building Connection & Community

It's no secret that reading books with children is a great way to connect, build memories, and instill a lifelong love of literature. Involving kids in book clubs fosters even greater literacy confidence by incorporating critical thinking skills and multiple learning modalities, all while strengthening family relationships and promoting community-building.

But in a society full of screens, activities, and other distractions, prioritizing reading and celebrating books can prove challenging. Even the most dedicated parents end up feeling overwhelmed by the hundreds of titles to choose from, not to mention the daunting task of sorting through activity ideas on the internet.

That's where we come in!

Our parent/child book club guides allow hosts to easily plan fun and interactive book club meetings—because we do all the work for you! For each of our curated book suggestions, we've compiled discussion questions, easy snack ideas, simple activities, and more.

Does your son love to plan? Give him this book and let him go for it! This not only empowers your son in his love of literacy–it also builds leadership skills and responsibility!

With our guides, kids will:
- Get off screens and into books
- Build friendships
- Learn empathy by reading a wide variety of stories
- Develop critical reading and thinking skills

Mother-Son book clubs benefit parents, too! Our guides will help parents:

- Prioritize reading time with reading goals and timelines
- Create a community around books and idea-sharing
- Build meaningful friendships
- Strengthen parent-child relationships
- Inspire a lifelong love of books, critical thinking, and connection

Who Can Use this Book

The *Mother-Son Book Club Guide* isn't just for mothers and sons! Fathers, daughters, homeschool parents, and all kinds of educators can benefit from the ideas we've included in this guide. We love it when librarians, storytime leaders, teachers, and book event planners have fun with our suggestions!

What's Included

Book Choices: These books are designed to appeal to 9-12 year olds. We recognize that this is a large age range, so we encourage facilitators to use careful judgment when deciding whether their son/group is ready for each book. While we offer book-specific age guides, each child is different and will respond as such.

Discussion Questions: Each book includes a list of questions to spark thought and discussion. Depending on the goals of your group, you may decide to focus on more intellectual or more "fun" questions. In any case, we hope the questions allow participants to practice critical thinking skills as they apply literary concepts to their life.

Activities: Activities are a great way to make literature fun and memorable! We've included a list of simple, book-related activities for each book. Feel free to use just one option, a few options, or to use our suggestions as a jumping-off point for your own ideas.

Snacks: What's a book club without snacks? For each book, we've included snack ideas that go along with the story. We couldn't include every food item mentioned in every book—those lists would be way too long!—but we've got plenty of creative ideas to get you started. Some snack suggestions relate to recipes that are included in the books themselves, while others may require an internet search.

Fun Facts: Each book includes interesting facts about the book and/or the author.

Picture Book Suggestions: Each book includes picture book suggestions. Use these to spark discussion by comparing and contrasting themes and topics found in the longer book. For example, after reading the book *Wonder*, reading a picture book about kids with special needs can help expand and deepen group discussion.

Tips for Launching YOUR Book Club

1. **Define Your Goals:** Every book club is different, and that's okay! Is your endgame to foster a love of reading, strengthen friendships and mother-son relationships, or to encourage good discussions? Being specific with your goals will help you focus on what success looks like for your group
2. **Find Participants:** Reach out to other moms with sons of a similar age—perhaps through a school class, church group, or other activity group. A group of 5-8 mother/son pairs is ideal, but feel free to include as few or as many people as you'd like!
3. **Choose Meeting Frequency:** Do you want to meet monthly, every six weeks, or every other month? Maybe every week in the summer? There's no wrong answer. Choose what works best for you!
4. **Create a Schedule:** Who will host each month? What day and time will you meet? Taking the time to plan about 3-6 months in advance makes a *huge* difference.
5. **Select Books:** There are many ways to do this, but these are our favorite methods:
    ◇ Vote on books for the whole year at once.
    ◇ Vote at the end of each meeting for the next month.
    ◇ Let the host family choose the next book.
6. **Communication:** Once your group is ready to get started, decide how to communicate important information. Some ideas include Evites, text messages, email, or social media groups. It's most helpful if one person is in charge of sending out info and reminders.
7. **Structure:** It's always a good idea to decide on a loose structure for each book club meeting. How much time do you hope to spend on discussion, snacks, and/

or activities? This way, hosts and guests know what to expect and can plan accordingly.
8. **Choose a Name for Your Book Club:** Get creative and have fun with this! Great names inspire fun and community!
9. **Be Flexible:** Life happens! Some meetings will be flawless, and some will be chaotic. Group members will come and go. People may not like the books you choose, you might forget the snack altogether, and there could even be some awkward social drama. Remind yourself that it's all part of the process, and imperfection is not only okay, but it often results in the best memories!

Tips for Hosts

1. Read through the book summaries and stats as you choose which books to read and when to read them. A grief book right before the holidays might not be the best experience, but a family-centered book could be perfect!
2. Prepare for book club meetings by reading through all the material for your chosen book in advance. Activity and snack planning may require an extra internet search and/or trip to the store, so give yourself time to prepare.
3. Let your creative juices flow! This is a guidebook, not a rule book. Always feel free to adapt our ideas to meet the needs of your group, and never resist allowing the ideas in this guidebook to inspire your own ideas. We'd love to hear about them—please share and tag us!

Activity Ideas for Any Book

- Make a movie trailer for the book
- Contact the author for a virtual book club visit
- Watch the movie (if there is one)
- Take a book club field trip: get creative with this idea, depending on which book you're reading and where you live
- Attend an author event
- Play book-themed Charades
- Make bookmarks based on the book
- Make character puppets
- Act out favorite scenes from the book
- Draw or paint favorite scenes or characters in the book
- Create a book collage with magazine clippings
- Plan a scavenger hunt for items related to the book
- Play book-themed Bingo
- "Cast" the characters with actual actors/celebrities

A Note from the Authors

When it comes to books, Stef and Meg have been connected for as long as they can remember.

As a child, Meg wrote all kinds of stories that her younger sister Stef eagerly gobbled up before begging for more. Stef's enthusiastic response helped propel Meg into a life of books, writing, and teaching. With a Masters degree in education and a career spanning secondary teaching, tutoring, freelance writing, and professional editing, Meg is passionate about helping kids and teens love literature and writing—and helping them believe they can create it, too!

By the time Stef became a mom, her bookish enthusiasm meant her house was stacked to the brim with books and reading. So when her eight-year-old daughter declared she hated reading, Stef was horrified! To entice her social butterfly back into the world of books, Stef launched her first Mother-Daughter book club with themed snacks and activities. That decision was a game-changer—and later led to additional years of Mother-Son book clubs with her four sons.

Stef has hosted everything from Mother-Daughter and Mother-Son book clubs to church and friend book clubs, in addition to earning multiple Masters degrees in literacy-related subjects. She and Meg have cheered each other on as they've continued to work together as writing partners, business partners, friends, and sisters.

Now that Meg's sons are in middle school, it seemed perfectly appropriate to partner once again—this time to publish their first Mother-Son Book Club Guide together! We hope you will love this guide. In creating this project, our overarching goal has always been to help moms and sons cultivate connection, community, and lasting memories of bookish joy.

And if you have a daughter, be sure to check out our Mother-Daughter Book Club Guide!

PART II

The Guide

Ground Zero
by Alan Gratz

On September 11, 2001, nine-year-old Brandon accompanies his father to work at the World Trade Center. When Brandon sneaks away to the shopping center, the tower is struck by a plane, separating Brandon from his dad and thrusting him into a fight for his life. In 2019, eleven-year-old Reshmina lives in a remote Afghan village caught between the Taliban and American forces. When she chooses to help a wounded American soldier, she puts her entire village in danger and must make an unthinkable sacrifice to protect her family. Through alternating chapters, *Ground Zero* explores courage, survival, and the far-reaching complexities and consequences of war.

Gratz, Alan. *Ground Zero*. New York: Scholastic Press, 2021.

STATS
- Publisher: Scholastic Press
- Originally Published: February 2, 2021
- Genre: Historical Fiction
- Subgenre: 9/11
- Themes: Survival, Impact of War, Resilience
- Page Count: 336
- Best for Ages: 10-12

AWARDS & LISTS
- #1 New York Times Bestseller
- Michigan Great Lakes Great Books Award
- Pennsylvania Young Reader's Choice Award

DISCUSSION QUESTIONS

1. Brandon changes a lot throughout the book. How does he change from the morning train ride to his escape from the towers? After Reshmina rescues him? After Reshmina's village is destroyed?
2. In what ways are Brandon and Reshmina different? In what ways are they similar?
3. Why do you think Reshmina risked her family's safety to help Taz, even though she hated American soldiers?
4. After Reshmina's village is destroyed, she says to Taz, "You can't help us by rebuilding villages and destroying them at the same time. Look at you. . . You can't even help me with both hands right now because your gun keeps getting in the way" (299). Is Taz's presence helpful or harmful to the villagers?
5. Why do you think Reshmina and her twin brother, Pasoon, developed such different ways of thinking? How do you handle disagreements with people you love?
6. When Reshmina confronts Taz about the damage Americans have caused, he says, "My dad once told me a bully is somebody who does whatever they want and never gets in trouble for it. Maybe that's what we are. Maybe we're the bullies" (301). What makes a person or nation a bully, and what prevents them from becoming one?
7. Why do you think Gratz chose to tell this story from two points of view and two different time periods?
8. Both Brandon and Reshmina experienced terrifying situations. What helped them survive and move forward?
9. In the caves near their village, Reshmina stumbles upon a collection of historical items. Think of your own history– what items are precious to you or your family?
10. Revenge is a powerful theme in the book. Which characters seek it, and why? At the end, Reshmina will never see her brother again "as long as Pasoon chose revenge" (304). Why does she choose a different path?

SNACK IDEAS
- **Bananas and pink grapefruit:** Eat foods to match the smells that led Brandon out of the underground mall
- **Fruit cookie:** Decorate it like an American flag or an Afghanistan flag
- **Rice Krispie Towers:** Make Rice Krispie treats, then stack and shape them to look like the Twin Towers
- **Afghan food:** naan, rice, and meat
- **Fruit skewers:** Use strawberries, bananas, and blueberries for red, white, and blue skewers

ACTIVITY IDEAS
- **Family Stories:** Interview family members about where they were on 9/11 and what their experience was like. Record their responses and share the stories with the group!
- **9/11 Memorial & Museum Tour:** Visit in-person or take a virtual tour.
- **Write Letters:** Send letters to police officers, firemen, nurses, or servicemen in your area to thank them for their service to your community.
- **Afghan Culture:** Each child chooses one aspect of Afghan culture to research and share with the group through a poster or short presentation.
- **Service Project:** Organize a local service project: ideas include making care packages for first responders, cleaning up a local park, or volunteering at a senior center.

FUN FACTS
- Alan Gratz wrote his first book in 5th grade, called *Real Kids Don't Eat Spinach*.
- Gratz has published over twenty novels, graphic novels, and novellas for kids.
- Gratz spends more time researching his historical novels than actually writing them!

IF YOU LIKED THIS BOOK, YOU'LL LOVE...
- *Hatchet* by Gary Paulsen
- *All Thirteen: The Incredible Cave Rescue of the Thai Boys' Soccer Team* by Christina Soontornvat

PICTURE BOOK SUGGESTIONS
- *September 11 We Will Never Forget* by Peter Benoit
- *Branches of Hope: The 9/11 Survivor Tree* by Ann Magee

Ground Zero
Planning Guide

Meeting Date & Time: _____

Host: _____

Rating: ☆☆☆☆☆

Thoughts about the Book:

_____

_____

_____

Snacks:

_____

_____

_____

Activities:

_____

_____

_____

Supplies Needed:

_____

_____

_____

Notes:

_____

_____

_____

How Did It Go?

_____

_____

_____

Future Planning

Next Book: _____
Next Meeting Time: _____
Next Host: _____

Nathan Hale's Hazardous Tales: One Dead Spy

by Nathan Hale

Nathan Hale is a terrible spy—duped and captured on his very first mission! But as he waits on the gallows, he's swallowed by a magical history book that spits him back out to tell his hangman and an attending British provost tales of history before he's gone for good. He begins with none other than his own life story, complete with descriptions of the Battle of Bunker Hill, the siege of Boston, the takeover of Fort Ticonderoga, and, of course, his very own tragic end. With humorous commentary and plenty of little-known details, this graphic novel begins the story of the Revolutionary War.

Hale, Nathan. *One Dead Spy: A Revolutionary War Tale*. New York: Amulet Books, 2012.

STATS
- Publisher: Amulet Books
- Originally Published: August 1, 2012
- Genre: Graphic Novel
- Subgenre: Nonfiction, History, Action, Adventure
- Themes: Patriotism, Sacrifice, War, Courage
- Page Count: 128
- Best for Ages: 8-12

AWARDS & LISTS
- #1 New York Times Bestseller
- Bluebonnet Award
- Black-Eyed Susan Award

DISCUSSION QUESTIONS

1. In his famous last words, Nathan Hale declares, "I regret that I have but one life to give for my country" (11). What makes this sentence powerful enough to last through the ages?
2. Why do you think the author chose Nathan Hale as the narrator of this story? How does telling his story to the hangman and the British provost enhance the book's entertainment factor?
3. Sacrifice is a major theme in the story. What do the American rebels and British soldiers give up? Is there anything you believe in strongly enough to die for?
4. Why do you think the author included humor in a story about serious events? How can humor help us cope with and/or understand difficult topics?
5. When the American rebels need someone to spy on the British, no one volunteers—until Nathan Hale steps forward to say, "I'm not ashamed to sneak and spy for my country" (86). Why do you think he is willing to do the job no one else wants to do?
6. The book includes many historical figures, such as Henry Knox, Ethan Allen, George Washington, Thomas Knowlton, Robert Rogers, Stephen Hempstead, and Benjamin Tallmadge. Which of these characters do you relate to most, and why?
7. The Americans lack supplies, shelter, and training, yet still win the war. What traits help them succeed, and what examples from the book show this?
8. What does it mean to be patriotic? Do you think patriotism is important? Why or why not?
9. Which battle do you remember the most in the book? Why does it stand out to you?
10. Nathan Hale is caught on his first mission—so why is he still seen as an American hero? What makes someone a hero, and which other characters fit that role?

SNACK IDEAS
- **Forage for food:** Ideas include dandelions or wild berries
- **Cook a meal over the fire**
- **Serve daily rations:** Bread, beef, milk, and vegetables
- **Fire cakes:** Use flour and water to make these historical biscuits
- **Shoe soup:** Carve potatoes to look like shoes and boil them in a watery soup

ACTIVITY IDEAS
- **Marching:** Practice marching in formation.
- **Card Games:** Play a card game, like the Revolutionary soldiers did when Nathan Hale wasn't around to slice the deck in two!
- **Comics:** Create an original comic about a historical event or an event that happened in your own life history.
- **Weapons:** Learn about different types of weapons used in the Revolutionary War.
- **Secret Mission:** Pretend to be spies and complete a secret mission. Secret missions could include a scavenger hunt, door dash, or acts of service.

FUN FACTS
- The author Nathan Hale shares the same name with the spy Nathan Hale!
- There are twelve books in the Hazardous Tales series, with more on the way.
- Nathan Hale (the author) started his illustration career by drawing simple cartoons.

IF YOU LIKED THIS BOOK, YOU'LL LOVE...
- *Ground Zero* by Alan Gratz
- *New Kid* by Jerry Craft

PICTURE BOOK SUGGESTIONS
- *The American Revolution: A Visual History* by DK and Smithsonian Institution
- *George vs. George: The Revolutionary War as Seen from Both Sides* by Rosalyn Schanzer

One Dead Spy
Planning Guide

Meeting Date & Time: _____

Host: _____

Rating: ☆☆☆☆☆

Thoughts about the Book:

_____

_____

_____

Snacks:

_____

_____

_____

Activities:

_____

_____

_____

Supplies Needed:

_____

_____

_____

Notes:

_____

_____

_____

How Did It Go?

_____

_____

_____

Future Planning

Next Book: _____
Next Meeting Time: _____
Next Host: _____

Ghost
by Jason Reynolds

Castle Cranshaw calls himself "Ghost," a nickname born the night Castle and his mom ran from his dad, who pulled a gun on them. Even though his father went to jail, Ghost has continued to carry a scream bottled up inside of him and it keeps getting him into trouble. When he stumbles upon an elite track practice, Coach invites him to join the team on one condition: Ghost has to stay out of trouble. Despite worn-out sneakers, school bullies, and the shadows of his past, Ghost must learn to outrun more than just his competition—he needs to defeat his own demons.

Reynolds, Jason. *Ghost*. New York: Atheneum, 2016.

STATS
- Publisher: Atheneum
- Originally Published: August 30, 2016
- Genre: Realistic Fiction
- Subgenre: Sports, Coming-of-Age
- Themes: Courage, Trauma, Friendship
- Page Count: 192
- Best for Ages: 10-12

AWARDS & LISTS
- New York Times Bestseller
- National Book Award for Young People's Literature Finalist

DISCUSSION QUESTIONS

1. Why does Castle choose the nickname "Ghost"? Does it fit him? Do you have a nickname? How did you get it?
2. Ghost has complicated feelings about his dad. Sometimes he wishes his dad would stay in jail forever, and other times he misses him. What is it about his dad that he misses? Why does he want his dad to stay in jail?
3. Ghost says, "Like for me, the best way to describe it is, I got a lot of scream inside" (p. 34). Have you ever felt like you had a lot of "scream" inside? What are some healthy ways to let those feelings out?
4. Ghost always thought he was a basketball player, so he's surprised to find out he's a talented sprinter. Have you ever discovered something new about yourself that surprised you?
5. When Coach asks the new track kids to share something no one else knows, how does it bring the team closer? Now try it—what's something most people don't know about you?
6. Near the end of the book, Coach tells Ghost: "...you can't run away from who you are, but what you can do is run toward who you want to be" (p. 155). What do you think this means?
7. Why is being on a team important to Ghost? What helps him bond with his teammates? In your own life, what strengthens your connections with family, sports teams, or school groups?
8. Why does Ghost steal the shoes? Do you think Coach handled the situation fairly by not telling Ghost's mom, while making him apologize and clean out the car?
9. The book starts and ends with a gunshot, but they serve very different purposes. Why do you think Jason Reynolds chose to structure the book this way?
10. Do you think Ghost wins the race at the end? Does it matter?

SNACK IDEAS
- **Sunflower seeds**
- **Chicken wings**
- **Chocolate milk**
- **Salisbury steak**
- **Chinese food**
- **Bacon and eggs**

ACTIVITY IDEAS
- **Track Practice:** Run races!
- **Stretching:** Learn common stretches runners use to warm up.
- **World Records:** Research world records and report on your favorites. Decide which world record you would want to break.
- **Trust Falls:** Take turns falling backwards while the group catches you to build unity and trust.
- **Running Shoes:** Design your own running shoes and give them a name.

FUN FACTS
- *Ghost* is the first book in the Track series. The other books are *Patina*, *Sunny*, and *Lu*.
- Jason Reynolds started out as a poet before writing novels.
- The idea for *Ghost* came from a similar situation that happened to one of Reynolds's friends.

IF YOU LIKED THIS BOOK, YOU'LL LOVE...
- *The Crossover* by Kwame Alexander
- *All Thirteen: The Incredible Cave Rescue of the Thai Boys' Soccer Team* by Christina Soontornvat

PICTURE BOOK SUGGESTIONS
- *Girl Running* by Annette Bay Pimental
- *Fauja Singh Keeps Going* by Simran Jeet Singh

Part 2: The Guide

Ghost
Planning Guide

Meeting Date & Time: _____

Host: _____

Rating: ☆☆☆☆☆

Thoughts about the Book:

_____

_____

_____

Snacks:

_____

_____

_____

Activities:

_____

_____

_____

Supplies Needed:

_____

_____

_____

Notes:

_____

_____

_____

How Did It Go?

_____

_____

_____

Future Planning

Next Book:_____

Next Meeting Time:_____

Next Host:_____

Wonder
by R.J. Palacio

August Pullman is the ugliest kid in the 5th grade. No, really. Thanks to multiple genetic anomalies, he'll never look like everyone else. So when Auggie decides to attend public school for the first time, it's the kind of decision that will change his life—and the lives of the people in his orbit. August, his friends, and his family members take turns narrating as Auggie faces bullies, the lunchroom, and betrayal, as well as the kindness he needs to survive his first year at Beecher Prep.

Palacio, R.J. *Wonder*. New York: Alfred A. Knopf, 2012.

STATS
- Publisher: Knopf Books for Young Readers
- Originally Published: February 14, 2012
- Genre: Realistic Fiction
- Subgenre: Diversity, Disabilities, Friendship
- Themes: Self-acceptance, Kindness, Bullying, Courage
- Page Count: 320
- Best for Ages: 9-12

AWARDS & LISTS
- #1 New York Times Bestseller
- ALA Notable Children's Book
- Amazon Best Book of the Year
- Barnes & Noble Best Book of the Year

DISCUSSION QUESTIONS

1. How did you feel about the book's structure? What do the different perspectives reveal about Auggie and his impact on those around him?
2. Auggie's parents encourage him to attend Beecher Prep, even though he doesn't want to. Have your parents ever encouraged you to try something you didn't want to do?
3. Why did Auggie cut off his braid after the first day of school? Why was it such a big deal, especially for Via?
4. Auggie says, "I wish every day could be Halloween. We could all wear masks all the time. Then we could walk around and get to know each other before we got to see what we looked like under the masks" (p. 73). Do you ever feel this way? How often do we judge people by appearance rather than who they are?
5. Via knows August is the "sun" her family revolves around, and Auggie understands why kids stare or say cruel things—but it still hurts. When Auggie resists going back to school, Via says, "The point is we all have to put up with the bad days" (p. 115). How do you handle tough days or hard situations?
6. Jack hurts Auggie on Halloween by saying something mean behind his back. Should Auggie have accepted Jack's apology? Why or why not?
7. Auggie often wonders if people are kind to him because they truly like him or just feel sorry for him. Is there a difference? What does it mean to be a true friend?
8. Why do you think some of the boys who used to bully Auggie end up standing up for him during the class trip? What caused them to change?
9. How does Auggie change from the beginning of the book to the end? What events or people help him grow the most?
10. One of the major themes of the book is to "choose kind." What does it mean to choose kindness in your life?

SNACK IDEAS
- **American cheese on whole wheat bread**
- **Graham crackers**
- **Juice boxes**
- **Saltines**
- **Frothy chocolate milk**
- **Apples, cut in pieces**
- **Grapes, cut in half**

ACTIVITY IDEAS
- **Notebook with Precepts:** Give everyone a notebook to write down their own precept. Share them with each other or create a club poster with all the precepts!
- **Point of View Activity:** Play a game or do a simple team-building activity. After the game, ask everyone to write a paragraph about what happened to them during the game. Compare how different everyone's point of view is.
- **Choose Kind:** Make "Choose Kind" t-shirts, buttons, or banners.
- **Awards:** Give each child their own special award.
- **Music:** Listen to the many songs referenced in the book! Feel free to dance!
- **Self-Portraits:** Choose an animal to represent you and draw a self-portrait as that animal.

FUN FACTS
- *Wonder* was inspired by an experience R.J. Palacio had with her three-year-old son when they met a little girl with a facial deformity.
- *Wonder* started a movement called "Choose Kind"—a campaign to teach kids to be kind and prevent bullying.
- R. J. Palacio is a Star Wars fan, just like Auggie!

IF YOU LIKED THIS BOOK, YOU'LL LOVE...
- *New Kid* by Jerry Craft
- *Holes* by Louis Sachar

PICTURE BOOK SUGGESTIONS
- *My Extraordinary Face* by Marissa Suchyta
- *Emmanuel's Dream: The True Story of Emmanuel Ofosu Yeboah* by Laurie Ann Thompson

Wonder
Planning Guide

Meeting Date & Time: _____

Host: _____

Rating: ☆☆☆☆☆

Thoughts about the Book:

_____

_____

_____

Snacks:

_____

_____

_____

Activities:

_____

_____

_____

Supplies Needed:

_____

_____

_____

Notes:

_____

_____

_____

How Did It Go?

_____

_____

_____

Future Planning

Next Book: _____
Next Meeting Time: _____
Next Host: _____

Fablehaven
by Brandon Mull

When Kendra and Seth arrive at their reclusive grandparents' estate for a two-week stay, they have no idea they're entering Fablehaven, a secret magical preserve filled with both wondrous and dangerous creatures. As the truth unfolds, the siblings are both enchanted and intimidated by the varied creatures they meet. And when Seth's curiosity leads to chaos during the Midsummer Eve festival, it's up to Fablehaven's newest arrivals to set things right before the magical world and their own family fall into ruin.

Mull, Brandon. *Fablehaven*. Salt Lake City: Shadow Mountain, 2006.

STATS
- Publisher: Shadow Mountain
- Originally Published: June 14, 2006.
- Genre: Fantasy
- Subgenre: Coming-of-Age, Adventure, Mythical Creatures
- Themes: Family, Good and Evil, Courage, Responsibility
- Page Count: 384
- Best for Ages: 8-12

AWARDS & LISTS
- New York Times Bestseller
- Young Reader's Choice Award

DISCUSSION QUESTIONS

1. Seth's emergency survival kit includes a cereal box filled with a compass and binoculars, among other things. What would you include in your own kit?
2. When Seth first goes into the woods, he's frightened by a porcupine. He says, "Though he dreaded admitting it, he wished Kendra had come. The porcupine would have made her scream, and her fear would have increased his bravery" (p. 35). How can the reactions of others influence how we feel in scary situations?
3. If you saw a witch in the woods, would you: A) spy on her, B) keep your distance and stay silent, or C) run home and tell Grandpa Sorenson? Why?
4. Were the fairies justified in attacking Seth and turning him into a walrus? Why or why not?
5. When Seth asks Dale why they can't look out the window on Midsummer's Eve, Dale replies, "Smart people learn from their mistakes. But the real sharp ones learn from the mistakes of others" (p. 152). Have you ever learned from someone else's mistake, or do you usually learn the hard way?
6. Would you look out the window on Midsummer's Eve or follow Grandpa's instructions? Why? Do you think Grandpa's rules were too strict?
7. How was Seth's recklessness both helpful and dangerous? Was Kendra's obedience helpful or not helpful?
8. Which magical creatures at the preserve did you find most interesting or frightening? Which would you most like to meet?
9. How does Fablehaven explore the difference between good and evil? Which creatures or characters are more complicated than they first seem to be?
10. Kendra sees Seth as brave but shows bravery herself. How do their styles compare? What does true bravery mean to you?

SNACK IDEAS
- **Cream of Wheat with raspberry preserves**
- **Chocolate rose buds**
- **Milk:** Drink from pie tins
- **Hot chocolate**
- **Beef stew**
- **Peanut butter and jelly sandwiches**

ACTIVITY IDEAS
- **Scavenger Hunt:** Gather a bunch of locks and set up a scavenger hunt where everyone has to find keys. Then have them figure out which locks the keys belong to for a prize!
- **Paint by Number:** Purchase or create your own paint by number canvases.
- **Exploring:** Go exploring in the woods and look for signs of mythical creatures.
- **Monsters:** Create your own monster out of clay or recycled materials.
- **Midsummer's Eve Festival:** Hold your own festival, but make it good instead of evil. Enjoy food and backyard games!

FUN FACTS
- *Fablehaven* is the first book in the Fablehaven series. There are five books total. There is also a follow-up series called Dragonwatch, with Kendra and Seth as the main characters.
- *Fablehaven* has been published in more than 30 foreign languages.
- Brandon Mull calls himself a kinetic thinker. This means he likes to squeeze stress balls and pop bubble wrap while he thinks!

IF YOU LIKED THIS BOOK, YOU'LL LOVE...
- *Sal and Gabi Break the Universe* by Carlos Hernandez
- *Holes* by Louis Sachar

PICTURE BOOK SUGGESTIONS
- *The Book of Mythical Beasts and Magical Creatures* by Stephen Krensky
- *The Bedtime Book of Magical Creatures* by Stephen Krensky

Fablehaven
Planning Guide

Meeting Date & Time: _____

Host: _____

Rating: ☆☆☆☆☆

Thoughts about the Book:

_____

_____

_____

Snacks:

_____

_____

_____

Activities:

_____

_____

_____

Supplies Needed:

_____

_____

_____

Notes:

_____

_____

_____

How Did It Go?

_____

_____

_____

Future Planning

Next Book: _____
Next Meeting Time: _____
Next Host: _____

Sal and Gabi Break the Universe

by Carlos Hernandez

All Sal wants is to fit in at his new school, quirky Culeco Academy, and to stop accidentally tearing holes in the universe. But blending in and keeping the multiverse intact is proving difficult, even for a budding magician like Sal. Labeled a bruja for his magical tricks and on the verge of cosmic disaster, Sal teams up with Gabi, the fast-talking, big-hearted student body president. Together, they must figure out how to contain the cosmic chaos before the multiverse and their lives spiral out of control.

Hernandez, Carlos. *Sal and Gabi Break the Universe*. Los Angeles: Disney-Hyperion, 2019.

STATS
- Publisher: Rick Riordan Presents
- Originally Published: March 5, 2019
- Genre: Fantasy
- Subgenre: Science Fiction, Diversity, Adventure
- Themes: Grief, Friendship, Family, Responsibility
- Page Count: 400
- Best for Ages: 9-12

AWARDS & LISTS
- Pura Belpré Award
- Nebula Award
- ALSC Notable Children's Books

DISCUSSION QUESTIONS

1. At the beginning of the book, Sal says, "You never know when the world is going to need a little magic" (3). What does this tell us about Sal's personality?
2. Sal says, "My first impulse was to talk smack about Mr. Lynott, be funny, make Octavio laugh and therefore like me. But half a second's pause and I knew that's not how you treat people, especially not people who are trying to do better" (45). Why do you think Sal is so aware of how he treats others and their feelings?
3. Gabi has a big, complex family with many dads. What does the word "family" mean to Gabi and her dads? How does her family make other people feel?
4. When Sal opens a portal, unintended consequences follow. How does he handle them, and what does this teach us about the ripple effects of our actions?
5. Would you like to attend Culeco Academy? Why or why not?
6. Sal and Gabi are very different. Do these differences strengthen or weaken their friendship? How can you tell?
7. How does Sal's diabetes affect his personality and the way he navigates life?
8. American Stepmom says, "The sooner you ask the people you love to lend you a hand, the easier life becomes. . . . Trust in the people who love you. We can all figure it out together" (229). Is it easy or hard to ask for help? Why?
9. To meditate, Sal imagines sleeping on a giant's belly, while Gabi imagines being inside a flying taco. What would you imagine to help you relax?
10. At the beginning of the book, Sal wants to bring his mother back from another universe. How does his view change by the end of the story?

SNACK IDEAS
- **Skittles**
- **Bananas, cashews, and cheese sticks**
- **Plantains**
- **Cuban Feast**
- **Rocky road ice cream:** bonbons, melted peanut butter, sprinkles, whipped cream, Skittles, and sparklers
- **Hot chocolate:** Sugar-free, with a sugar-free mint

ACTIVITY IDEAS
- **Magic Tricks:** Learn to perform a magic trick!
- **Knitting:** Learn how to knit a scarf.
- **Hospital Volunteer:** Take a field trip to volunteer at a children's hospital. If that's not possible, make cards or paint rocks and deliver to people who need a smile!
- **Design an AI Robot:** Using paper, clay, or recyclable materials, design a robot. What kind of personality would it have?
- **Multiverse You:** Design yourself from another universe. What would be the same? What would be different?

FUN FACTS
- Gabi and Sal were originally adult characters in Hernandez's short stories.
- There is a sequel to this book called *Sal and Gabi Fix the Universe*.
- Carlos Hernandez has a PhD in English and creates educational learning games.

IF YOU LIKED THIS BOOK, YOU'LL LOVE...
- *Fablehaven* by Brandon Mull
- *Holes* by Louis Sachar

PICTURE BOOK SUGGESTIONS
- *You'll Find Me* by Amanda Rawson Hill
- *Magic Tricks with Coins, Cards, and Everyday Objects* by Jake Banfield

Sal and Gabi Break the Universe
Planning Guide

Meeting Date & Time: _____

Host: _____

Rating: ☆☆☆☆☆

Thoughts about the Book:

_____

_____

_____

Snacks:

_____

_____

_____

Activities:

_____

_____

_____

Supplies Needed:

_____

_____

_____

Notes:

_____

_____

_____

How Did It Go?

_____

_____

_____

Future Planning

Next Book: _____
Next Meeting Time: _____
Next Host: _____

Hatchet
by Gary Paulsen

Thirteen-year-old Brian is flying to visit his father in the Canadian wilderness when the pilot of the small plane suffers a fatal heart attack, leaving Brian to crash-land alone. With nothing but his clothes and a hatchet, he must learn to survive in the wild. As Brian builds a shelter, finds food, and faces the dangers of nature, he grows stronger and more resourceful. But as winter approaches and no rescue comes, he realizes surviving will take more than just skill.

Paulsen, Gary. *Hatchet*. New York: Bradbury Press, 1987.

STATS
- Publisher: Bradbury Press
- Originally Published: September 1987
- Genre: Classic
- Subgenre: Realistic Fiction, Action/Adventure, Survival
- Themes: Survival, Self-reliance, Coming-of-Age, Man vs. Nature
- Page Count: 192
- Best for Ages: 9-12

AWARDS & LISTS
- Newbery Honor 1988
- Dorothy Canfield Fisher Children's Book Award

DISCUSSION QUESTIONS

1. Brian is stranded in the wilderness with only a hatchet. If you were stranded and could only bring one item to help you survive, what would it be and why?
2. How would the story have changed if Brian had found the plane's survival pack at the beginning? How would the story have changed if Brian didn't have the hatchet?
3. After Brian is attacked by the porcupine, the book says this is "when he learned the most important rule of survival, which was that feeling sorry for yourself didn't work" (77). How does feeling sorry for himself make Brian's life harder? How can you channel feelings of disappointment in healthy ways?
4. We've lost many wilderness survival skills in our modern world. What kinds of skills do you need to survive in today's society?
5. What role does fire play in the story, both practically and symbolically? Why is fire so important to Brian's survival—and his confidence?
6. After learning how to catch fish, Brian says "he could feel a new hope building in him. Not hope that he would be rescued—that was gone. But hope in his knowledge... Tough hope" (120). How can knowledge bring us hope?
7. Is nature Brian's enemy or friend? How does it challenge him, and how does it help him survive?
8. Why do you think Brian is able to survive for so long on his own? If he hadn't been rescued, do you think he would have survived the winter?
9. Brian decides not to tell his dad about his mom's affair, and he never brings it up with his mom either. Why do you think he makes this decision? What would you have done?
10. How does Brian change by the end of the book? What does he learn about himself, and how has his experience transformed him?

SNACK IDEAS
- **Gut cherries** (choke cherries)
- **Raspberries**
- **Turtle eggs** (pretend chicken eggs are turtle eggs)
- **Fish:** bluegills, sunfish, and perch
- **Peach whip**
- **Orange Tang**

ACTIVITY IDEAS
- **Survival Skills:** Learn how to build a shelter, forage for food, and build a fire.
- **Hike:** Go on a hike or camp in the wilderness.
- **Bow & Arrow:** Learn how to construct a bow and arrow and/or practice shooting one.
- **Spear Throwing:** Use a long stick as a spear and have a contest to see who can throw it the farthest.
- **Survival Kits:** Make personal survival kits for wilderness adventures or emergency kits for at-home preparation.

FUN FACTS
- Gary Paulsen spent a lot of time in the woods and used his own experience with survival to write this book.
- *Hatchet* is the first in a series of five books, called Brian's Saga.
- Gary Paulsen wrote over 200 books for kids.

IF YOU LIKED THIS BOOK, YOU'LL LOVE...
- *All Thirteen: The Incredible Cave Rescue of the Thai Boys' Soccer Team* by Christina Soontornvat
- *Ground Zero* by Alan Gratz

PICTURE BOOK SUGGESTIONS
- *Bushcraft Kid* by Dan Wowak
- *Lonely Planet Kids Kids' Survival Guide: Practical Skills for Intense Situations* by Ben Hubbard

Hatchet
Planning Guide

Meeting Date & Time: _____

Host: _____

Rating: ☆☆☆☆☆

Thoughts about the Book:

_____

_____

_____

Snacks:

_____

_____

_____

Activities:

_____

_____

_____

Supplies Needed:

_____

_____

_____

Notes:

_____

_____

_____

_____

How Did It Go?

_____

_____

_____

Future Planning

Next Book: _____
Next Meeting Time: _____
Next Host: _____

New Kid

by Jerry Craft

Jordan Banks dreams of attending art school in New York City. Instead, his parents enroll him in an elite private school where he's one of the few students of color. As Jordan navigates new friends, school bullies, and all kinds of teachers, he struggles to stay connected to his neighborhood friends and personal identity. Caught between two worlds, Jordan seeks to find where he truly belongs and who he wants to be.

Craft, Jerry. *New Kid*. New York: Harper, 2019.

STATS
- Publisher: Quill Tree Books
- Originally Published: February 5, 2019
- Genre: Graphic Novel
- Subgenre: Realistic Fiction, Coming-of-Age, Diversity
- Themes: Prejudice, Racism, Standing Up for Yourself
- Page Count: 256
- Best for Ages: 9-12

AWARDS & LISTS
- Newbery Winner, 2020
- Coretta Scott King Author Award
- Kirkus Prize for Young Readers Literature

DISCUSSION QUESTIONS

1. Have you ever been the new kid? What makes being new especially challenging?
2. Jordan says, "Fitting in on the ride to school is hard work! I have to be like a chameleon" (56). Have you ever felt like you had to change to fit in?
3. Jordan draws cartoons to process strong emotions. How does this help him, and what do you do to understand your feelings?
4. After dinner with his grandfather, Jordan says, "It took me a few days to realize Grandpa's story was a metaphor... I decided to see if General Tso's Chicken could get along with Pepper Steak" (118). Have you tried to bring people together from different parts of your life? What went well? What challenges did you face?
5. The book highlights microaggressions that minorities face, like being called the wrong name or having assumptions made about food or interests. How do these microaggressions affect Jordan and Drew?
6. Jordan, Kirk, Liam, Drew, Alex, and Maury are very different, but they still get along. How are your friends different from you? How are you similar?
7. Some of Jordan's teachers are supportive, while others are not. Have you had a bad teacher? How did you handle it? What makes a good teacher?
8. Why did Jordan share Alex's story about the hand puppet? Was that the right choice? Have you ever hidden something about yourself for fear of what others think?
9. What stereotypes appear in the story, and how do the characters challenge them? How can we avoid stereotyping others?
10. At the end of the book, Jordan's dad tells him that he looks like "a new kid," and Jordan agrees (245). How has the meaning of that phrase changed from the beginning of the story? How does Jordan grow and change?

SNACK IDEAS
- **Chinese food:** General Tso's chicken, shrimp lo mein, and pepper steak
- **Cookies decorated like basketballs**
- **KFC**
- **Sweet potato pie**
- **Crumb cake**

ACTIVITY IDEAS
- **Practice Handshakes:** Use Jordan's dad's tips to learn how to shake hands.
- **Play sports:** Get outside and play soccer, basketball, or baseball.
- **Draw/Write Comics:** Write or draw a comic based on a real-life experience or create an imaginative comic strip story. Feel free to work in pairs: take turns creating each panel, or assign one person to write the story while the other draws the comics.
- **Design Book Covers:** Design the book cover for a book about your life. What would you include? Share ideas with the group.
- **Gift Exchange:** Assign each person the name of someone who will be attending the book club. Ask them to bring a small gift for that person. During the party, exchange gifts and ask participants to share something kind or thoughtful about the person they were assigned.

FUN FACTS
- *New Kid* is the first graphic novel to win the Newbery Award. It's also the first book to win the Newbery, the Coretta Scott King Award, and the Kirkus Prize.
- *New Kid* was heavily inspired by Jerry Craft's experiences and those of his sons.
- *New Kid* is the first book in a series, with *Class Act* and *School Trip* as sequels.

IF YOU LIKED THIS BOOK, YOU'LL LOVE...
- *Nathan Hale's Hazardous Tales: One Dead Spy* by Nathan Hale
- *Sal and Gabi Break the Universe* by Carlos Hernandez

PICTURE BOOK SUGGESTIONS
- *The Day You Begin* by Jacqueline Woodson
- *The Invisible Boy* by Trudy Ludwig

New Kid
Planning Guide

Meeting Date & Time: _____

Host: _____

Rating: ☆☆☆☆☆

Thoughts about the Book:

_____

_____

_____

Snacks:

_____

_____

_____

Activities:

_____

_____

_____

Supplies Needed:

_____

_____

_____

Notes:

_____

_____

_____

How Did It Go?

_____

_____

_____

Future Planning

Next Book: _____

Next Meeting Time: _____

Next Host: _____

Holes
by Louise Sachar

When Stanley Yelnats is sent to Camp Green Lake for a crime he didn't commit—stealing a pair of famous shoes—he's not sure what to expect. But it's definitely not a dried-up lake bed with a warden who insists that campers dig holes all day. Stanley befriends a quiet boy named Zero, and through their friendship and the required digging, they begin to uncover long-buried secrets. When Zero attempts a daring escape, he and Stanley must come face-to-face with family curses, fate, and poisonous lizards if they're going to survive.

Sachar, Louis. *Holes*. New York: Farrar, Straus and Giroux, 1998.

STATS
- Publisher: Farrar, Straus & Giroux
- Originally Published: August 20, 1998
- Genre: Mystery
- Subgenre: Realistic Fiction, Adventure, Coming-of-Age
- Themes: Fate, Justice, Friendship, Family, Racism
- Page Count: 233
- Best for Ages: 9-12

AWARDS & LISTS
- Newbery Medal 1999
- National Book Award for Young People's Literature 1998
- Dorothy Canfield Fisher Children's Book Award
- William Allen White Children's Book Award

DISCUSSION QUESTIONS

1. Why do you think the Camp Green Lake boys give each other nicknames? If you were at Camp Green Lake, what would your nickname be?
2. What do you think is the scariest part of Camp Green Lake–the Warden, the poisonous lizards, the heat, the other boys, or something else?
3. Justice is a major theme in *Holes*, in both Stanley's storyline and Kissing Kate's storyline. Who received unjust punishments? Who did/didn't receive the justice they deserved?
4. Why do Stanley and Zero become friends? In what ways do they need each other, and how do they help each other grow?
5. When Stanley and Zero take off for God's Thumb, Stanley complains about his family curse. Zero replies, "When you spend your whole life living in a hole, the only way you can go is up" (160). What do you think this means?
6. Do you believe in family curses or that some people are just more lucky or unlucky than others? Why?
7. Family history and legacy play a big role in this book. How did Stanley's and Zero's ancestors affect their lives? How have the actions of your ancestors influenced you?
8. When Stanley first arrives at Camp Green Lake, he thinks he's unlucky that the shoes fell from the sky. But at the top of God's Thumb, he thinks, "It had to be destiny" (187). How often do things that seem unlucky or horrible end up turning out for the best? Can you think of an example from your own life?
9. Stanley grows stronger by digging holes, but how else does he change? How do the other characters change from the start to the end of their stories?
10. Were you surprised by how all the storylines came together in the end? How did you feel about the ending?

SNACK IDEAS
- **Sunflower seeds**
- **Onions**
- **Sploosh:** Canned peaches
- **Canteens:** Serve water in canteens
- **Dirt Pudding with mini shovels**
- **Donut Holes**

ACTIVITY IDEAS
- **Dig Holes:** Go outside to dig a hole! Though perhaps not five feet deep...
- **Treasure Hunt:** Hide "treasure" somewhere in your house (or outside) and give the boys a map to find the treasure.
- **Yellow Spotted Lizards Craft:** Make yellow spotted lizards out of air dry clay or recyclable materials.
- **Piggyback Relay:** Instead of carrying someone up a mountain, organize a relay race where the kids carry each other on their backs.
- **Name Game:** Have each child figure out what their name would be if their first name were spelled backwards.

FUN FACTS
- The setting of *Holes* was inspired by Louis Sachar's dislike of doing yardwork during hot Texas summers.
- Sachar is well known for his Wayside School book series, beginning with *Sideways Stories from Wayside School*.
- The Disney movie *Holes* is very similar to the book because Sachar wrote the screenplay himself.

IF YOU LIKED THIS BOOK, YOU'LL LOVE...
- *Ghost* by Jason Reynolds
- *Sal and Gabi Break the Universe* by Carlos Hernandez

PICTURE BOOK SUGGESTIONS
- *Sam & Dave Dig a Hole* by Mac Barnett
- *Stick and Stone* by Beth Ferry

Holes
Planning Guide

Meeting Date & Time: _____

Host: _____

Rating: ☆☆☆☆☆

Thoughts about the Book:

_____

_____

_____

Snacks:

_____

_____

_____

Activities:

_____

_____

_____

Supplies Needed:

_____

_____

_____

Notes:

_____

_____

_____

How Did It Go?

_____

_____

_____

Future Planning

Next Book: _____

Next Meeting Time: _____

Next Host: _____

The Crossover
by Kwame Alexander

Twin brothers Josh and Jordan are not only best friends, they're the stars of their middle school basketball team. Coached by their father, a retired pro, they've learned the rules of the game and of life both on and off the court. But everything changes when Jordan gets a girlfriend and drifts away from basketball, and Dad's health begins to decline. Without Jordan by his side, Josh faces jealousy, anger, and a growing sense of isolation as his emotions reach a dangerous tipping point. Then the unthinkable happens, and Josh must find a way to survive heartbreak in order to rebuild everything he's lost.

Alexander, Kwame. *The Crossover*. Boston: Houghton Mifflin Harcourt, 2014.

STATS
- Publisher: HMH Books for Young Readers
- Originally Published: March 18, 2014
- Genre: Novel in Verse
- Subgenre: Realistic Fiction, Grief, Sports Fiction
- Themes: Family, Trust, Responsibility
- Page Count: 240
- Best for Ages: 9-12

AWARDS & LISTS
- Newbery Award Winner, 2015
- Coretta Scott King Award Honor
- NCTE Charlotte Huck Honor Book
- Lee Bennett Hopkins Poetry Award

DISCUSSION QUESTIONS

1. Why do you think Kwame Alexander chose to write this book in verse (See Fun Facts for the actual answer!)? Did you like this format? Why or why not?
2. Josh calls his dreadlocks his "wings." What do they symbolize for him, and why is it such a big deal when he has to cut them off?
3. Josh faces a lot—Jordan's new girlfriend, losing his "wings," and Dad's illness. What emotions fuel his outburst at Jordan? Have you ever felt one way inside but acted differently on the outside?
4. How does Josh's view of his father change, and how does he cope with his loss? After their father's death, do you think the brothers will grow closer or drift apart? Why?
5. How is Josh's relationship with his mom different from his relationship with his dad? What role does each parent play in shaping who he is? How have your parents shaped you?
6. Josh's nickname on the court is Filthy McNasty. His dad's pro basketball nickname is "Da Man." Do you have sports nicknames? Regular nicknames? Where did they come from?
7. Basketball Rule #5 says, "When you stop playing your game, you've already lost" (93). What does this mean, and how does it apply to Josh's life?
8. Josh and Jordan are twins but very different. What adjectives describe each of them? What positive adjectives describe others in your book club?
9. The book is not only titled *The Crossover*, it ends with the following line: "I watch the ball leave his hands like a bird up high, skating the sky, crossing over us" (237). What are some meanings of "crossover" that are important in Josh's story?
10. How does Josh change by the end of the book? What did he learn about himself, his family, and growing up?

SNACK IDEAS
- **Basketball cupcakes or cookies**
- **Chinese food:** Egg rolls, dumplings, and wonton soup
- **Krispy Kreme donuts**
- **Sweet iced tea**
- **Vegetable lasagna**
- **Sweet potato pie**

ACTIVITY IDEAS
- **Play Basketball:** Go outside and shoot some hoops!
- **Poetry:** Try writing a free verse poem. Use one of the poems in the book as a starting point.
- **Nicknames:** Encourage everyone to create a fun nickname for themselves based on something they love—like sports, music, or gaming—and share it with the group!
- **Book of Rules:** Josh's dad shares Basketball Rules that double as life lessons. Create your own list of life rules, either individually or as a group.
- **Free Throw Contest:** Have a free throw contest or play knock-out with a basketball and hoop–or crumpled paper and a laundry basket!

FUN FACTS
- *The Crossover* series includes two other books. *Rebound* is a prequel and *Booked* is a companion novel about soccer.
- *The Crossover* was turned into a series on Disney+.
- Kwame Alexander chose to write *The Crossover* in verse because he felt that poetry mirrored the quick game of basketball.

IF YOU LIKED THIS BOOK, YOU'LL LOVE...
- *New Kid* by Jerry Craft
- *Ghost* by Jason Reynolds

PICTURE BOOK SUGGESTIONS
- *Dream Big: Michael Jordan and the Pursuit of Excellence* by Deloris Jordan
- *The Dreams We Made* by Lisa Bentley

The Crossover
Planning Guide

Meeting Date & Time: _____

Host: _____

Rating: ☆☆☆☆☆

Thoughts about the Book:

_____

_____

_____

Snacks:

_____

_____

_____

Activities:

_____

_____

_____

Supplies Needed:

_____

_____

_____

Notes:

_____

_____

_____

_____

How Did It Go?

_____

_____

_____

Future Planning

Next Book: _____
Next Meeting Time: _____
Next Host: _____

Part 2: The Guide

The Boy Who Harnessed the Wind
Young Readers Edition
by William Kamkwamba

Growing up in a small village in Malawi, Africa, William Kamkwamba's love for learning drives him to excel in school until his family can no longer afford the fees. Then a devastating famine strikes, and William's family faces the threat of starvation. Determined to exercise his mind, William reads books about wind energy and builds a windmill using scrap materials. Despite skepticism and community stigma, William's persistence and ingenuity lead to a life-changing breakthrough that transforms his family's future.

Kamkwamba, William, and Bryan Mealer. *The Boy Who Harnessed the Wind, Young Readers Edition*. Illustrated by Anna Hymas. New York: Dial Books for Young Readers, 2015.

STATS
- Publisher: Rocky Pond Books
- Originally Published: January 5, 2016
- Genre: Nonfiction
- Subgenre: Memoir, STEM, Survival, Coming-of-Age
- Themes: Resilience, Power of Education, Innovation, Community
- Page Count: 304
- Best for Ages: 9-12

AWARDS & LISTS
- Amazon Best Books of the Year 2012
- Junior Library Guild Selection 2012

DISCUSSION QUESTIONS

1. William is heartbroken when he can no longer attend school. How would you feel if you couldn't go to school anymore? What else do we take for granted?
2. What role does the famine play in William's life? What does it reveal about his character and resilience?
3. William experiences many hardships, especially when he has to kill his beloved dog. Do you think that was the right decision? What would you have done?
4. William's inventions often failed, sometimes with painful consequences. What helps him keep trying? Describe a time when you faced disappointment and kept trying.
5. William's community didn't always trust his decisions, in part because they didn't understand what William was learning. Why do you think people fear things they don't understand? How can you avoid this kind of behavior?
6. How does the windmill change life for William's family? How does electricity make your daily life better?
7. What does William's story teach us about invention and innovation?
8. William's mother jokes that he is like Noah, who built the ark. She says, "Everyone laughed at Noah, but look what happened" (274). People often laugh at William, but he never gives up. Have you ever been laughed at? How do you respond?
9. The book ends with William's advice: "If you want to make it, all you have to do is try" (p. 278). Describe something you tried to do, even if you were scared or overwhelmed at first. How did your experience turn out in the end?
10. What do you find most inspiring about William's story? In what ways did it impact or change you?

SNACK IDEAS
- **Potatoes**
- **Mangoes**
- **Maize**
- **Oatmeal porridge**
- **Boiled pumpkin leaves**
- **Meat, pastries, and fruits**

ACTIVITY IDEAS
- **Soccer Ball:** Make a soccer ball out of plastic grocery bags like William and his friends did.
- **Make a Windmill:** Design your own windmill using popsicle sticks. If possible, purchase a mini generator motor with a mini fan leaf, as well as LED light diodes made for science projects. Attach the generator wires to the light diode. Use a hair dryer to blow the blades of the windmill and watch the light glow!
- **Make a Pinwheel:** For a simpler activity, make a pinwheel out of paper, a pushpin, and a straw. When you blow on it, the pinwheel spins!
- **Invention Time:** Create your own invention out of recycled materials.
- **Electronics:** If you have access to old electronics, such as a radio, let the kids take it apart to learn how it works.

FUN FACTS
- William Kamkwamba travels the world telling his story, and he has inspired educational efforts across the globe.
- Kamkwamba's story was originally published as an adult book. Along with the Young Readers edition, there is also a picture book and a movie adaptation.
- Kamkwamba co-founded the Moving Windmills Project to bring innovative solutions to pressing needs in parts of Africa.

IF YOU LIKED THIS BOOK, YOU'LL LOVE...
- *Ground Zero* by Alan Gratz
- *Hatchet* by Gary Paulsen

PICTURE BOOK SUGGESTIONS
- *Lion Lights: My Invention That Made Peace with Lions* by Richard Turere
- *Iqbal and His Ingenious Idea* by Elizabeth Suneby

The Boy Who Harnessed the Wind
Planning Guide

Meeting Date & Time: _____

Host: _____

Rating: ☆☆☆☆☆

Thoughts about the Book:

_____

_____

_____

Snacks:

_____

_____

_____

Activities:

_____

_____

_____

Supplies Needed:

_____

_____

_____

Notes:

_____

_____

_____

How Did It Go?

_____

_____

_____

Future Planning

Next Book: _____
Next Meeting Time: _____
Next Host: _____

All Thirteen:
The Incredible Cave Rescue of the Thai Boys' Soccer Team
by Christina Soontornvat

When Coach Ek and thirteen members of his soccer team set out for a hike in Tham Luang cave, they had no idea that the rainy season was about to come early. In Thailand, the rainy season means months of rain and flooding, and within hours, their path out of the cave had disappeared underwater. Trapped for over a week without food or light, the boys' survival rested in the skill and ingenuity of cave divers, local experts, and rescue teams in collaboration with international military and government leaders. Thanks to the heroic efforts of so many, the boys' rescue became a story of courage, determination, and generosity that captured the world's attention.

Soontornvat, Christina. *All Thirteen: The Incredible Cave Rescue of the Thai Boys' Soccer Team.* Somerville, MA: Candlewick Press, 2020.

STATS
- Publisher: Candlewick
- Originally Published: October 13, 2020
- Genre: Nonfiction
- Subgenre: Adventure, Survival, Disasters
- Themes: Collaboration, Innovation, Family, Love, Survival
- Page Count: 288
- Best for Ages: 10-12

AWARDS & LISTS
- Newbery Honor, 2021

DISCUSSION QUESTIONS

1. Once the boys realize they are trapped, Coach Ek leads them in meditation: "Breath by breath, they each become the master of the one thing they can control inside Tham Luang: their own mind" (p. 55). Why do you think meditation helped the boys survive?
2. Why do you think so many people from around the world were willing to sacrifice their time and money to help rescue the boys?
3. At first, the people in charge didn't want to listen to the experienced cave divers about how dangerous the situation was, but then they changed their minds. What does this teach us about communication and what it means to be a good leader?
4. What qualities do you think helped the boys survive nine days in complete darkness with no food?
5. The experienced cave divers knew how dangerous the rescue mission was and how unlikely it was to succeed. Why do you think they were still willing to take the risk?
6. What does this story teach us about teamwork and the importance of exploring multiple solutions to a problem? How can we apply these lessons to our own experiences?
7. Who are the true heroes in this story? What makes someone a hero?
8. The book shares a lot about Thai culture. What role do you think culture played in both the boys' survival and the success of the rescue effort?
9. "Somehow, they have defied the terrible odds. This rescue was impossible, and they did it anyway" (p. 211). How does this statement inspire or impact you?
10. Instead of blaming Coach Ek for leading the boys into the cave, the boys' parents send a letter of trust and support. How might this have affected Coach Ek, and what can we learn from their response?

SNACK IDEAS
- **Beng-Beng:** The Thai boys' favorite candy bar (or something similar with crispy rice, caramel, and chocolate)
- **Gel packs**
- **MREs:** Ready-to-eat meals that include an entree, side dish, and dessert
- **Crispy pork, rice, and Japanese sushi**
- **KFC**

ACTIVITY IDEAS
- **Soccer:** Get outside and play a game of soccer.
- **Meditation:** Learn about meditation and then practice your new skills.
- **Darkness:** Find the darkest place in your house. Turn out all the lights and try to block any incoming light from windows or door cracks. Experience what it's like to be in complete darkness, and then talk about the experience together.
- **Caving:** Create a cave out of chairs and blankets. Encourage the kids to crawl from one end of the cave to the other.
- **Go on an Adventure:** Find an adventurous activity to do, such as rock climbing, kayaking, or hiking. Before you go, talk about safety and what precautions should be taken. Discuss what to do in an emergency.

FUN FACTS
- *All Thirteen* is the true story of a real-life rescue in 2018.
- Christina Soontornvat is of Thai descent, and she holds a degree in engineering.
- Soontornavat has won three Newbery Honor awards and is the only person to win honors for fiction and nonfiction in the same year.

IF YOU LIKED THIS BOOK, YOU'LL LOVE...
- *Hatchet* by Gary Paulsen
- *Ground Zero* by Alan Gratz

PICTURE BOOK SUGGESTIONS
- *When Beavers Flew: An Incredible True Story of Rescue and Relocation* by Kristen Tracy
- *The Light That Shines Forever: The True Story and Remarkable Rescue of 669 Children on the Eve of World War II* by David Warner

All Thirteen
Planning Guide

Meeting Date & Time: _____

Host: _____

Rating: ☆☆☆☆☆

Thoughts about the Book:

_____
_____
_____

Snacks:

_____
_____
_____

Activities:

_____
_____
_____

Supplies Needed:

_____

_____

_____

Notes:

_____

_____

_____

How Did It Go?

_____

_____

_____

Future Planning

Next Book: _____

Next Meeting Time: _____

Next Host: _____

Appendix

INDEX

Books By Genre
- Adventure
    - *Ground Zero* 13
    - *Nathan Hale's Hazardous Tales: One Dead Spy* 19
    - *Fablehaven* 37
    - *Sal and Gabi Break the Universe* 43
    - *Hatchet* 49
    - *Holes* 61
    - *All Thirteen* 79
- Classic
    - *Hatchet* 49
- Fantasy
    - *Fablehaven* 37
    - *Sal and Gabi Break the Universe* 43
- Graphic Novel
    - *Nathan Hale's Hazardous Tales: One Dead Spy* 19
    - *New Kid* 55
- Historical Fiction
    - *Ground Zero* 13
    - *Nathan Hale's Hazardous Tales: One Dead Spy* 19
- Nonfiction/Memoir
    - *The Boy Who Harnessed the Wind* 73
    - *All Thirteen* 79
- Novel in Verse
    - *The Crossover* 67
- Realistic Fiction
    - *Ghost* 25
    - *Wonder* 31
    - *Hatchet* 49
    - *New Kid* 55
    - *Holes* 61
    - *The Crossover* 67

Books By Topic

- Believing in Yourself
    - *Ghost* 25
    - *Sal and Gabi Break the Universe* 43
    - *Hatchet* 49
    - *New Kid* 55
- Bullying
    - *Ghost* 25
    - *Wonder* 31
    - *Sal and Gabi Break the Universe* 43
    - *New Kid* 55
    - *Holes* 61
- Coming-of-Age
    - *Ground Zero* 13
    - *Ghost* 25
    - *Wonder* 31
    - *Fablehaven* 37
    - *Sal and Gabi Break the Universe* 43
    - *Hatchet* 49
    - *New Kid* 55
    - *Holes* 61
    - *The Crossover* 67
- Community
    - *Ground Zero* 13
    - *The Boy Who Harnessed the Wind* 73
    - *All Thirteen* 79
- Courage
    - *Ground Zero* 13
    - *Nathan Hale's Hazardous Tales: One Dead Spy* 19
    - *Ghost* 25
    - *Wonder* 31
    - *Fablehaven* 37
    - *Hatchet* 49
    - *New Kid* 55

Appendix

- ◇ *Holes* 61
- ◇ *The Boy Who Harnessed the Wind* 73
- ◇ *All Thirteen* 79
- Disabilities
  - ◇ *Wonder* 31
  - ◇ *Sal and Gabi Break the Universe* 43
- Diversity
  - ◇ *Wonder* 31
  - ◇ *New Kid* 55
  - ◇ *Holes* 61
  - ◇ *The Crossover* 67
- Education
  - ◇ *Holes* 61
  - ◇ *The Boy Who Harnessed the Wind* 73
- Family
  - ◇ *Ground Zero* 13
  - ◇ *Ghost* 25
  - ◇ *Holes* 61
  - ◇ *Wonder* 31
  - ◇ *Fablehaven* 37
  - ◇ *Sal and Gabi Break the Universe* 43
  - ◇ *The Crossover* 67
  - ◇ *The Boy Who Harnessed the Wind* 73
- Friendship
  - ◇ *Ghost* 25
  - ◇ *Wonder* 31
  - ◇ *Sal and Gabi Break the Universe* 43
  - ◇ *New Kid* 55
  - ◇ *Holes* 61
  - ◇ *All Thirteen* 79
- Good vs Evil
  - ◇ *Fablehaven* 37
- Grief
  - ◇ *Sal and Gabi Break the Universe* 43
  - ◇ *The Crossover* 67

- History
  - *Ground Zero* 13
  - *Nathan Hale's Hazardous Tales: One Dead Spy* 19
- Humor
  - *Nathan Hale's Hazardous Tales: One Dead Spy* 19
  - *Sal and Gabi Break the Universe* 43
  - *New Kid* 55
- Impact of War
  - *Ground Zero* 13
  - *Nathan Hale's Hazardous Tales: One Dead Spy* 19
- Kindness
  - *Wonder* 31
  - *Sal and Gabi Break the Universe* 43
  - *New Kid* 55
  - *Holes* 61
  - *All Thirteen* 79
- Man vs. Nature
  - *Hatchet* 49
  - *Holes* 61
  - *The Boy Who Harnessed the Wind* 73
  - *All Thirteen* 79
- Patriotism
  - *Ground Zero* 13
  - *Nathan Hale's Hazardous Tales: One Dead Spy* 19
- Resilience
  - *Ghost* 25
  - *Wonder* 31
  - *Hatchet* 49
  - *New Kid* 55
  - *Holes* 61
  - *The Crossover* 67
  - *The Boy Who Harnessed the Wind* 73
  - *All Thirteen* 79
- Responsibility
  - *Ground Zero* 13
  - *Nathan Hale's Hazardous Tales: One Dead Spy* 19

Appendix

- ◇ *Fablehaven* 37
- ♦ Sacrifice
  - ◇ *Ground Zero* 13
  - ◇ *Nathan Hale's Hazardous Tales: One Dead Spy* 19
  - ◇ *The Boy Who Harnessed the Wind* 73
- ♦ Self-Acceptance
  - ◇ *Ghost* 25
  - ◇ *Wonder* 31
  - ◇ *New Kid* 55
  - ◇ *Holes* 61
  - ◇ *The Crossover* 67
- ♦ Self-Reliance
  - ◇ *Fablehaven* 37
  - ◇ *Hatchet* 49
  - ◇ *Holes* 61
  - ◇ *The Boy Who Harnessed the Wind* 73
  - ◇ *All Thirteen* 79
- ♦ Sports
  - ◇ *Ghost* 25
  - ◇ *New Kid* 55
  - ◇ *The Crossover* 67
- ♦ STEM
  - ◇ *Sal and Gabi Break the Universe* 43
  - ◇ *The Boy Who Harnessed the Wind* 73
  - ◇ *All Thirteen* 79
- ♦ Survival
  - ◇ *Ground Zero* 13
  - ◇ *Hatchet* 49
  - ◇ *Holes* 61
  - ◇ *The Boy Who Harnessed the Wind* 73
  - ◇ *All Thirteen* 79
- ♦ Trauma
  - ◇ *Ghost* 25

ABOUT THE AUTHORS

Meghan Voss, M.Ed.

Meghan Voss loves reading, teaching, and helping kids write! She earned a B.A. in English from Brigham Young University and a Masters in Secondary Education from the University of Maryland. A former high school English teacher, Meghan has published magazine articles and blog posts, edited everything from dissertations to picture books, and currently works as an education manager with a local non-profit organization. When Meghan isn't geeking out over books and literature, you can find her lifting weights, hiking, and picking fresh huckleberries for homemade pie. Meghan lives in northwest Montana with her husband, three children, and the occasional bear that strolls through her backyard.

Stefanie Hohl, M.Ed., MFA

Stefanie Hohl loves books, book clubs, and writing books for kids! She is the author of *The Remember Tree*, *Where is the Star*, and the ABC See, Hear, Do series, a learn to read program that uses movement to teach early reading skills. She has a Masters in Education in Curriculum and Instruction from Penn State, as well as a Masters of Fine Arts in Writing for Children and Young Adults from Vermont College of Fine Arts. When Stefanie isn't planning book clubs for her kids, she loves to run, snowboard, and bake peanut butter bars. Stefanie lives in Pittsburgh with her husband, five children, two very silly dogs, and two cuddly cats.

www.ingramcontent.com/pod-product-compliance
Lightning Source LLC
Chambersburg PA
CBHW070942080526
44589CB00013B/1606